In **1935** if you wanted to
read a good book, you needed
either a lot of money or a library card.
Cheap paperbacks were available, but their
poor production generally mirrored the quality
between the covers. One weekend that year,
Allen Lane, Managing Director of The Bodley Head,
having spent the weekend visiting Agatha Christie,
found himself on a platform at Exeter station trying to
find something to read for his journey back to London.
He was appalled by the quality of the material he had to
choose from. Everything that Allen Lane achieved from that
day until his death in 1970 was based on a passionate belief
in the existence of 'a vast reading public for *intelligent*
books at a low price'. The result of his momentous vision
was the birth not only of Penguin, but of the 'paperback
revolution'. Quality writing became available for the price of
a packet of cigarettes, literature became a mass medium
for the first time, a nation of book-borrowers became a
nation of book-buyers – and the very concept of book
publishing was changed for ever. Those founding
principles – of quality and value, with an overarching
belief in the fundamental importance of reading –
have guided everything the company has
done since 1935. Sir Allen Lane's
pioneering spirit is still very much alive
at Penguin in 2005. Here's to
the next 70 years!

MORE THAN A BUSINESS

'We decided it was time to end the almost customary half-hearted manner in which cheap editions were produced – as though the only people who could possibly want cheap editions must belong to a lower order of intelligence. We, however, believed in the existence in this country of a vast reading public for intelligent books at a low price, and staked everything on it'
Sir Allen Lane, 1902–1970

'The Penguin Books are splendid value for sixpence, so splendid that if other publishers had any sense they would combine against them and suppress them'
George Orwell

'More than a business … a national cultural asset'
Guardian

'When you look at the whole Penguin achievement you know that it constitutes, in action, one of the more democratic successes of our recent social history'
Richard Hoggart

Death in the Bunker

IAN KERSHAW

PENGUIN BOOKS

PENGUIN BOOKS

Published by the Penguin Group
Penguin Books Ltd, 80 Strand, London WC2R ORL, England
Penguin Group (USA) Inc., 375 Hudson Street, New York, New York 10014, USA
Penguin Group (Canada), 10 Alcorn Avenue, Toronto, Ontario, Canada M4V 3B2
(a division of Pearson Penguin Canada Inc.)
Penguin Ireland, 25 St Stephen's Green, Dublin 2, Ireland
(a division of Penguin Books Ltd)
Penguin Group (Australia), 250 Camberwell Road, Camberwell, Victoria 3124,
Australia (a division of Pearson Australia Group Pty Ltd)
Penguin Books India Pvt Ltd, 11 Community Centre,
Panchsheel Park, New Delhi – 110 017, India
Penguin Group (NZ), cnr Airborne and Rosedale Roads, Albany,
Auckland 1310, New Zealand (a division of Pearson New Zealand Ltd)
Penguin Books (South Africa) (Pty) Ltd, 24 Sturdee Avenue,
Rosebank 2196, South Africa

Penguin Books Ltd, Registered Offices: 80 Strand, London WC2R ORL, England

www.penguin.com

Hitler 1936–1945: Nemesis first published by Allen Lane 2000
Published in Penguin Books 2001
This extract published as a Pocket Penguin 2005

1

Copyright © Ian Kershaw, 2000
All rights reserved

The moral right of the author has been asserted

Set in 11/13pt Monotype Dante
Typeset by Palimpsest Book Production Limited
Polmont, Stirlingshire
Printed in England by Clays Ltd, St Ives plc

The atmosphere in the bunker on 20 April 1945, Hitler's fifty-sixth birthday, was more funereal than celebratory. There was no trace of the pomp and circumstance of earlier years. The gaunt ruins of the Reich Chancellery were themselves a stark reminder, if one was needed, that there was no cause for celebration. Hitler felt this himself. His birthday with the Russians at the gates of Berlin was – everything points to this – an embarrassment to him, and for all those who were obliged to offer him their birthday greetings.

Traditionally, Hitler's personal staff gathered to be the first to offer their congratulations on the stroke of midnight. This year, Hitler, in depressed mood, had already told his valet, Heinz Linge, that he did not want to receive his household; there were no grounds for congratulation. Linge was ordered to pass on the message. Predictably, this Führer order was ignored. Waiting in the ante-room, as midnight approached, to offer their formal congratulations were Chief Adjutant General Wilhelm Burgdorf, Himmler's liaison SS-Gruppenführer Hermann Fegelein (who had recently married Eva Braun's sister, Gretl), the long-serving factotum Julius Schaub, who had been a member of the 'household' since the mid-1920s, Hitler's adjutants

NSKK-Oberführer Alwin-Broder Albrecht and SS-Sturmbannführer Otto Günsche, Ribbentrop's liaison Walter Hewel, and press officer Heinz Lorenz. Hitler, tired and dejected, said Linge should inform them that he had no time to receive them. Only following Fegelein's intercession with his sister-in-law Eva Braun (who had returned to the Reich Chancellery some weeks earlier, announcing she was staying with Hitler, and resisting all attempts to persuade her to leave) did he concede, trudging down the assembled line of his staff to receive their murmured birthday greetings with a limp handshake and a vacant expression. Further muted, almost embarrassed, congratulations followed from the military leaders attending the first briefing of the day. Afterwards, Hitler drank tea in his study with Eva Braun. It was approaching nine o'clock in the morning before he finally went to bed, only to be disturbed almost immediately by General Burgdorf with the news of a Soviet breakthrough and advance towards Cottbus, some sixty miles south-east of Berlin, on the southern part of the front. Hitler took the news standing in his nightshirt at the door of his bedroom, and told Linge he had not slept up to then and to waken him an hour later than normal, at 2 p.m.

After breakfasting, playing with his alsatian puppy for a while, and having Linge administer his cocaine eyedrops, he slowly climbed the steps into the Reich Chancellery park. Waiting with raised arms in the Nazi salute were delegations from the Courland army, from the SS-Division 'Berlin', and twenty boys

from the Hitler Youth who had distinguished themselves in combat. Was this what Berlin's defence relied
upon? one of Hitler's secretaries wondered. Hitler
muttered a few words to them, patted one or two
on the cheek, and within minutes left them to carry
on the fight against Russian tanks.

Bormann, Himmler, Goebbels, Reich Youth
Leader Artur Axmann, and Dr Morell were among
those in a further line waiting to be received at the
door of the Chancellery's Winter Garden. Looking
drained and listless, his face ashen, his stoop
pronounced, Hitler went through the motions of a
brief address. Not surprisingly, he was by now incapable of raising spirits. Lunch with Christa Schroeder
and senior secretary Johanna Wolf was a depressing
affair. Afterwards, he retraced his steps down into the
bowels of the earth for the late afternoon briefing. He
would not leave the bunker again alive.

By now, most of the leading figures in the Reich
– at least, those in the Berlin vicinity – were assembled. Göring, Dönitz, Keitel, Ribbentrop, Speer, Jodl,
Himmler, Kaltenbrunner, the new Chief of Staff
General Hans Krebs, and others all presented their
greetings. No one spoke of the looming catastrophe.
They all swore their undying loyalty. Everyone
noticed that Göring had discarded his resplendent
silver-grey uniform with gold-braided epaulettes for
khaki – 'like an American general', as one participant
at the briefing remarked. Hitler passed no comment.

I

The imminent assault on Berlin dominated the briefing. The news from the southern rim of the city was catastrophic. Göring pointed out that only a single road to the south, through the Bayerischer Wald, was still open; it could be blocked at any moment. His chief of staff, General Karl Koller, added that any later attempt to transfer the High Command of the Wehrmacht by air to new head-quarters could be ruled out. Hitler was pressed from all sides to leave at once for Berchtesgaden. He objected that he could not expect his troops to fight the decisive battle for Berlin if he removed himself to safety. Keitel had told Koller before the briefing that Hitler was determined to stay in Berlin. When greeting Hitler, Keitel had murmured words to the effect that they had confidence that he would take urgent decisions before the Reich capital became a battleground. It was a strong hint that Hitler and his entourage should leave for the south while there was still time. Hitler interrupted, saying: 'Keitel, I know what I want. I will fight on in front of, within, or behind Berlin.' Nevertheless, Hitler now seemed indecisive. Increasingly agitated, he declared moments later that he would leave it to fate whether he died in the capital or flew at the last moment to the Obersalzberg.

There was no indecision about Göring. He had sent his wife Emmy and daughter Edda to the safety of the Bavarian mountains more than two months earlier. He had written his will in February. Crate-loads of his looted art treasures from Carinhall, his palatial country residence in the Schorfheide, forty miles north of Berlin, had been shipped south in March. Half a million marks were transferred to his account in Berchtesgaden. By the time he arrived at the Reich Chancellery to pass on his birthday wishes to Hitler, Carinhall was mined with explosives; his own remaining belongings were packed and loaded on to lorries, ready to go on to the Obersalzberg. Göring lost no time at the end of the briefing session in seeking out a private word with Hitler. It was urgent that he go to southern Germany, he said, to command the Luftwaffe from there. He needed to leave Berlin that very night. Hitler scarcely seemed to notice. He muttered a few words, shook hands absent-mindedly, and the first paladin of the Reich departed, hurriedly and without fanfare. It seemed to Albert Speer, standing a few feet away, to be a parting of ways that symbolized the imminent end of the Third Reich.

It was the first of numerous departures. Most of those who had come to proffer their birthday greetings to Hitler and make avowals of their undying loyalty were waiting nervously for the moment when they could hasten from the doomed city. Convoys of cars were soon heading out of Berlin north, south, and west, on any roads still open. Dönitz left for the north, armed with Hitler's instructions – the implementation of the directive five days earlier on division of command should the Reich be geographically split – to take over the leadership in the north and continue the struggle. It was a sign of Dönitz's high standing with Hitler on account of his uncompromising support for the stance of fighting to the last, and of hopes for a continuation of the U-boat war, that he was given plenipotentiary powers to issue all relevant orders to State and Party, as well as to the Wehrmacht in the northern zone. Himmler, Kaltenbrunner, and Ribbentrop soon followed. Speer left later that night in the direction of Hamburg, without any formal farewell.

Hitler, according to Julius Schaub's post-war testimony, was deeply disappointed at the desire of his paladins to leave the bunker in barely concealed haste. He gave no more than a perfunctory nod of valediction to those who, now that his power was as good as ended, were anxious to save what they could of themselves and their possessions. By this time, most of the army top-brass had left. And Bormann had already told the remaining government ministers – Finance Minister Lutz Graf Schwerin-Krosigk, Transport Minister Julius Dorpmüller, Justice

Minister Otto Georg Thierack, Minister for the Occupied Eastern Territories (a long redundant post) Alfred Rosenberg, Education Minister Bernhard Rust, and Labour Minister Franz Seldte – together with head of the Presidential Chancellery, the old survivor, Otto Meissner, to make hasty preparations to leave for the south, since the road would soon be blocked. Hitler's naval adjutant, Admiral Karl-Jesko von Puttkamer, was dispatched to the Obersalzberg to destroy important papers there. His two older secretaries, Johanna Wolf and Christa Schroeder, were summoned to his study that evening and told to be ready to leave for the Berghof within the hour. Four days earlier, he had told them in confident tones: 'Berlin will stay German. We must just gain time.' Now, he said, the situation had changed so much in the past four days, that he had to break up his staff.

The scene in the courtyard of the Reich Chancellery was near-chaotic as vehicles were stuffed with bags and suitcases, the rumble of artillery a reminder of how close the Red Army was as the cars hurried through the night, through clouds of smoke billowing from burning buildings, past shadowy ruins and Volkssturm men setting up street barricades, to waiting aeroplanes. During the following three nights, some twenty flights were made from Gatow and Staaken aerodromes in Berlin, taking most of Hitler's staff to Berchtesgaden.

Late in the evening, the remaining adjutants, secretaries, and his young Austrian diet cook, Constanze Manziarly, gathered in his room for a drink with Hitler and Eva Braun. There was no talk here of the war. Hitler's youngest secretary, Traudl Junge, had been shocked to hear him admit for the first time in her presence earlier that day that he no longer believed in victory. *He* might be ready to go under; her own life, she felt, had barely begun. Once Hitler – early for him – had retired to his room, she was glad to join Eva Braun, and other bunker 'inmates', even including Bormann and Morell, in an 'unofficial' party in the old living room on the first floor of Hitler's apartment in the Reich Chancellery. In the ghostly surrounds of a room stripped of almost all its former splendour, with the gramophone scratching out the only record they could find – a schmaltzy pre-war hit called 'Red Roses Bring You Happiness' ('*Blutrote Rosen erzählen Dir vom Glück*') – they laughed, danced, and drank champagne, trying to enjoy an hour or two of escapism – before a nearby explosion sharply jolted them back to reality.

When Hitler was awakened at 9.30 next morning, it was to the news that the centre of Berlin was under artillery fire. He was at first incredulous, immediately demanding information from Karl Koller, Luftwaffe chief of staff, on the position of the Soviet artillery battery. An observation post at Berlin's zoo provided the answer: the battery was no more than eight miles away in the suburb of Marzahn. The dragnet was closing fast. The information scarcely helped to calm

Hitler's increasingly volatile moods. As the day wore on, he seemed increasingly like a man at the end of his tether, nerves ragged, under intense strain, close to breaking point. Irrational reactions when a frenzy of almost hysterically barked-out orders proved impossible to implement or demands for information impossible to supply, point in this direction.

Soon, he was on the telephone again to Koller, this time demanding figures of German planes in action in the south of the city. Communications failures meant Koller was unable to provide them. Hitler rang once more, this time wanting to know why the jets based near Prague had not been operational the previous day. Koller explained that enemy fighters had attacked the airfields so persistently that the jets had been unable to take off. 'Then we don't need the jets any more. The Luftwaffe is superfluous,' Hitler had replied in fury. 'The entire Luftwaffe leadership should be hanged straight away!'

II

The drowning man clutched at yet another straw. The Soviets had extended their lines so far to the north-east of Berlin that it opened up the chance, thought Hitler and Chief of Staff Krebs, for the Panzer Corps led by SS-Obergruppenführer Felix Steiner to launch a counter-attack with good chances of success. A flurry of telephone calls with more than a hint of near-hysteria assigned a motley variety of remaining units, including naval and Luftwaffe forces untrained in ground warfare and without heavy armour, to Steiner's command. 'Every commander withholding forces has forfeited his life within five hours,' Hitler screamed at Koller. 'The commanders must know that. You yourself guarantee with your head that the last man is deployed.' Any retreat to the west was strictly forbidden to Steiner's forces. Officers unwilling to obey were to be shot immediately. 'On the success of your assignment depends the fate of the German capital,' Hitler told Steiner – adding that the commander's life also hinged on the execution of the order. At the same time, Busse's 9th Army, to the south of Berlin, was ordered to restabilize and reinforce the defensive line from Königswusterhausen to Cottbus. In addition, aided by a northward push of parts of Schörner's Army Group Centre, still doggedly fighting in the vicinity of Elsterwerda, around sixty miles south of Berlin, it was to attack and cut off Konev's tank forces that had broken through to their rear. It was an illusory hope. But Hitler's false optimism was still being pandered to by some of the generals. His mood visibly brightened after hearing upbeat reports from his most recent field-marshal, Schörner (who had been promoted on 5 April), and from General Wenck about the chances of his newly constructed 12th Army attacking American forces on the Elbe.

Colonel-General Heinrici, Commander of Army

Group Vistula, was not one of the eternal optimists who played to Hitler's constant need for good news. He warned of encirclement if the 9th Army were not pulled back. He threatened resignation if Hitler persisted in his orders. But Hitler did persist; and Heinrici did not resign. The general had implied to Speer days earlier that Berlin would be taken without serious resistance. This thinking was anathema to Hitler. He told Jodl on the day his orders to Steiner and to the 9th Army went out: 'I will fight as long as I have a single soldier. When the last soldier deserts me, I will shoot myself.' Late that night, he still exuded confidence in Steiner's attack. When Koller told him of the inadequacies of the Luftwaffe troops he had been compelled to supply to Steiner's forces, Hitler replied: 'You will see. The Russians will suffer the greatest defeat, the bloodiest defeat in their history before the gates of the city of Berlin.'

It was bravado. Two hours earlier, Dr Morell had found him drained and dejected in his study. The doctor and his medications, however little efficacious in an objective sense, had been for years an important psychological prop for Hitler. Now, Morell wanted to give him a harmless further dose of glucose. Without any forewarning, Hitler reacted in an uncontrollable outburst, accusing Morell of wanting to drug him with morphine. He knew, he said, that the generals wanted to have him drugged so that they could ship him off to Berchtesgaden. 'Do you take me for a madman?'

Hitler railed. Threatening to have him shot, he furiously dismissed the quivering doctor.

The storm had been brewing for days. It burst on the afternoon of 22 April, during the briefing that began at 3.30 p.m. Even as the briefing began, Hitler looked haggard, stony-faced, though extremely agitated, as if his thoughts were elsewhere. He twice left the room to go to his private quarters. Then, as dismaying news came through that Soviet troops had broken the inner defence cordon and were within Berlin's northern suburbs, Hitler was finally told – after a frantic series of telephone calls had elicited contradictory information – that Steiner's attack, which he had impatiently awaited all morning, had not taken place after all. At this, he seemed to snap. He ordered everyone out of the briefing room, apart from Keitel, Jodl, Krebs, and Burgdorf. Even for those who had long experience of Hitler's furious outbursts, the tirade which thundered through the bunker for the next half an hour was a shock. One who witnessed it reported that evening: 'Something broke inside me today that I still can't grasp.' Hitler screamed that he had been betrayed by all those he had trusted. He railed at the long-standing treachery of the army. Now, even the SS was lying to him: after Sepp Dietrich's failure in Hungary, Steiner had not attacked. The troops would not fight, he ranted, the anti-tank defences were down. As Jodl added, he also knew that munitions and fuel would shortly run out.

Hitler slumped into his chair. The storm subsided. His voice fell to practically a whimper. The war was lost, he sobbed. It was the first time any of his small audience had heard him admit it. They were dumbstruck. He had therefore determined to stay in Berlin, he went on, and to lead the defence of the city. He was physically incapable of fighting himself, and ran the risk of falling wounded into the hands of the enemy. So he would at the last moment shoot himself. All prevailed upon him to change his mind. He should leave Berlin forthwith and move his headquarters to Berchtesgaden. The troops should be withdrawn from the western front and deployed in the east. Hitler replied that everything was falling apart anyway. He could not do that. Göring could do it. Someone objected that no soldier would fight for the Reich Marshal. 'What does it mean: fight?' asked Hitler. 'There's not much more to fight for, and if it's a matter of negotiations the Reich Marshal can do that better than I can.'

At this, Hitler, his face a deathly pallor, left the briefing room and retreated to his own quarters. He sent for his remaining secretaries, Gerda Christian and Traudl Junge, and his dietician Constanze Manziarly. Eva Braun was also present as he told his staff they should get ready; a plane would take them south in an hour. 'It's all lost,' he said, 'hopelessly lost.' (*Es ist alles verloren, hoffnungslos verloren.*) Somewhat to their own surprise, his secretaries found themselves rejecting the offer to leave and telling

Hitler that they would stay with him in the bunker. Eva Braun had already told Hitler she was not leaving.

Urgent telephone calls were meanwhile put through from Dönitz and Himmler. Neither could persuade him to change his mind. Ribbentrop arrived. He was not even allowed to see Hitler. Goebbels was also present. Hitler, highly disturbed, had telephoned him around five o'clock, raving about treachery, betrayal, and cowardice. Goebbels hurried as fast as he could go to the bunker, and spoke a while alone with Hitler. He was able to calm him down. Goebbels emerged to announce that on the Führer's orders, he, his wife, and his children would be moving into the bunker and living there from now on. For the Propaganda Minister, Hitler's decision was the logical consequence of his consistent stance; he saw it in full pathos as a historic deed which determined the heroic end in Berlin of a latter-day Siegfried, betrayed by all around him.

For hard-headed military men like Karl Koller, the perspective was very different: Hitler was abandoning the German people at the time of their greatest need; he had renounced his responsibility to armed forces, state, and people at the most critical moment; it was dereliction of duty worse than many offences for which draconian retribution had been meted out.

There were indeed serious practical considerations following from Hitler's hysterical behaviour. He had simply said he was staying in Berlin. The others should leave and go where they wanted. He had no further orders for the Wehrmacht. But he was still supreme commander. Who was now to give orders? Berlin was doomed for certain within a few days. So where were Wehrmacht Headquarters to be? How could forces simply be withdrawn from the western front without any armistice negotiations? After fruitless pleading with Hitler, Keitel decided to travel to the headquarters of General Wenck's 12th Army. Hitler had finally agreed to sign an order to Wenck to abandon his previous operational plans – defending against the Americans on the Elbe – and march on Berlin, linking up with the remnants of the 9th Army, still fighting to the south of the city. The aim was to cut off enemy forces to the south-west of the capital, drive forward 'and liberate (*freikämpfen*) again the Reich capital where the Führer resides, trusting in his soldiers'. Wenck's army had been hastily put together at the beginning of April. It was inadequately armed; its panzer support was weak; and many of its troops were poorly trained. They were outnumbered by the Soviet troops facing them, and possessed only a quarter of the weaponry. What Wenck was supposed to do in the unlikely event of breaking through to the centre of Berlin – other than bringing out Hitler, if need be by force (as Keitel later put it) – was left entirely unclear.

Hitler, his equilibrium now temporarily restored, was solicitous enough to make sure that Keitel was well fed before he set out on his journey. Jodl was meanwhile to take steps to ensure that part of the High Command of the Wehrmacht was immediately transferred to Berchtesgaden, while the remainder would be moved to the barracks at Krampnitz, near Potsdam. Hitler's overall direction would remain intact, maintained through telephone links to Krampnitz and Berchtesgaden. The regular briefings would continue, though with reduced personnel.

In the bunker, meanwhile, Hitler had ordered Schaub to burn all the papers and documents in his private safe in the bunker. He was afterwards instructed to do the same in Munich and at the Berghof. After a perfunctory farewell from the master he had served for twenty years, he left Berlin and flew south. The bunker company had by now shrunk. Those left behind consoled themselves with drink. They referred to the bunker as 'the mortuary' and its inmates as 'a show house of living corpses'. Their main topic of conversation was when and how to commit suicide.

Remarkably, Hitler had regained his composure by the next morning. He was still venting anger at troops that seemed to have evaporated into thin air. 'It's so disgraceful,' he fumed. 'When you think about it all, why still live!' But Keitel's news about his meeting with Wenck had provided yet another glimmer of hope. Hitler ordered all available troops, however ill-equipped, to be added to Wenck's army. Dönitz had already been cabled the previous evening to have all available sailors as the most urgent priority, overriding all naval concerns, flown to Berlin to join the 'German battle of fate (*deutsche Schicksalsschlacht*)' in the Reich capital. Telegrams were also dispatched to Himmler, and to Luftwaffe high command to send their remaining reserves to aid the reinforcement of Berlin. 'The enemy knows I'm here,' Hitler added, referring to Goebbels's proclamation to the Berlin people that day, telling them that the Führer would remain in the city to lead its defence. They would concentrate all their efforts on taking the capital as soon as possible. But that, thought Hitler, gave him a chance to lure them into the trap of Wenck's army. Krebs reckoned they still had four days. 'In four days the business has to be decided,' agreed Hitler.

That afternoon, Albert Speer arrived back in the bunker. He had had a tortuous ten-hour journey to cover only 100 or so miles from the Hamburg area. He had quickly given up an attempt to drive along roads choked with refugees desperate to leave Berlin by any route still open, and flew first to the airfield at Rechlin in Mecklenburg, then on to Gatow aerodrome in the west of Berlin. There, he picked up a Fieseler Storch light aircraft, eventually navigating a landing on the East-West Axis approaching the Brandenburg Gate, the wide boulevard on which he had triumphantly paraded six years earlier during Hitler's fiftieth birthday celebrations, now, its lampposts removed, converted into a makeshift landing-strip. For weeks, Speer had been working with industrialists and generals to sabotage Hitler's 'scorched earth' orders. Only two days earlier, in Hamburg, he had recorded an address – never, in the event, broadcast, and probably made with more than one eye on embellishing his own prospects in a world after Hitler – urging an end to the pointless destruction. But despite the growing alienation, Speer could still not break free of Hitler. The emotional bonds remained strong. After his unsung departure on the evening of Hitler's birthday, the former Armaments Minister felt unhappy at ending their special relationship without an appropriate farewell. That was the reason for his wholly unnecessary, extremely hazardous flight back into the cauldron.

On his way to Hitler's room in the bunker, he encountered Bormann. Not anxious to end his own days in the bunker catacombs, the Secretary to the Führer implored Speer to use his influence to persuade Hitler to leave for the south. It was still just possible. In a few more hours it would be too late. Speer gave a non-committal reply. He was then ushered in to see Hitler, who, as Bormann had foreseen, lost no time in asking Speer's opinion whether he should stay in Berlin or fly to Berchtesgaden. Speer did not hesitate. It would be better to end his life as Führer in the Reich capital than in his 'weekend house', he said. Hitler looked tired, apathetic, resigned, burnt out. He had decided to stay in Berlin, he murmured. He had just wanted to hear Speer's opinion. As the previous day, he said he would not fight. There was the danger that he would be captured alive. He was also anxious to avoid his body falling into the hands of his enemy to be displayed as a trophy. So he had given orders to have his body burnt. Eva Braun would die alongside him. 'Believe me, Speer,' he added, 'it will be easy to end my life. A brief moment, and I am freed from everything, released from this miserable existence.'

Minutes later, in the briefing – by now a far smaller affair, over much more quickly, and, because of communications difficulties, often lacking precise, up-to-date intelligence – Hitler, immediately after speaking of his imminent death and cremation, was again trying to exude optimism. Only now did Speer realize how much of an act the role of Führer had always been.

All at once, there was a commotion in the corridor. Bormann hurried in with a telegram for Hitler. It was from Göring. The report of the momentous meeting the previous day, which Koller had personally flown to Berchtesgaden to deliver verbally, had placed the Reich Marshal in a quandary. Koller had helped persuade a hesitant Göring that, through his actions, Hitler had in effect given up the leadership of state and Wehrmacht. As a consequence, the edict of 29 June 1941, nominating Göring as his successor in the event of his incapacity to act, ought to come into force. Göring was still unsure. He could not be certain that Hitler had not changed his mind, and he worried about the influence of his arch-enemy, Bormann.

Eventually, Koller suggested sending a telegram. Göring agreed. Koller, advised by Lammers, drafted its careful wording, cautiously stipulating that, had Göring not heard by ten o'clock that evening, he would presume that the terms of the succession law would come into operation, and that he would take over the entire leadership of the Reich. He would take immediate steps, he told Koller, to surrender to the western powers, though not to the Russians.

His telegram to Hitler (with a copy to Below, the Luftwaffe adjutant still in the bunker) gave no inkling of disloyalty. But, as Göring had feared, Bormann was immediately at work to place the worst possible construction upon it. Hitler seemed at first unconcerned, or apathetic. But when Bormann produced another telegram from Göring, summoning Ribbentrop to see him immediately, should he have received no other directive from Hitler or himself by midnight, it was an easy matter to invoke the spectre of treachery once more. Bormann was pushing at an open door. For months, Goebbels (and Bormann himself) had been the most prominent among those urging Hitler to dismiss Göring, portrayed as an incompetent, corrupt, drug-taking sybarite, single-handedly responsible for the débâcle of the Luftwaffe and the air-superiority of the Allies which they saw as so decisive for Germany's plight. Given Hitler's extreme volatility, as the events of the previous day had demonstrated only too plainly, the uncontrolled torrent of rage at Göring's ruination of the Luftwaffe, his corruption, and his morphine addiction was utterly predictable.

Savouring his victory, Bormann swiftly drew up a telegram, stripping Göring of his rights of succession, accusing him of treason, but refraining from further measures if the Reich Marshal resigned all his offices forthwith on health grounds. Göring's agreement was received within half an hour. But that evening, the once most powerful man in the Reich after Hitler was nevertheless put under house-arrest, the Berghof surrounded by SS guards. Hitler's power was fading fast; but it was not yet finally at an end.

Late that night, before leaving the bunker, Speer sat in Eva Braun's room, drinking a bottle of Moët et Chandon and eating cakes and sweets. Eva seemed calm and relaxed. She told Speer that Hitler had wanted to send her back to Munich, but she had refused; she had come to Berlin to end it. At three in the morning, Hitler appeared. Speer felt emotional at saying farewell. He had flown back to the bunker precisely for this purpose. It was, for him, a poignant moment. Hitler proffered a weak handshake. 'You're going then. Good. Good-bye.' That was all.

Another visitor besides Speer had arrived in the bunker unannounced the previous evening: General Helmuth Weidling, commander of the 56th Panzer Corps, attached to the 9th Army fighting to the southeast of Berlin. Communications had been lost with him since the evening of 20 April, and Hitler had ordered him arrested for desertion. Astonishingly, he had made his way back to Berlin, and into the Führer Bunker to protest his innocence. Hitler was impressed. Next morning, he made Weidling responsible for Berlin's defence, replacing Colonel Ernst Kaether, who had held the post for all of two days.

It was a daunting assignment. Weidling had at his disposal units rapidly patched together, comprising 44,600 soldiers, along with 42,500 Volkssturm men (whose fighting capabilities were severely limited on account both of their age and their miserable equipment), around 2,700 boys from the Hitler Youth, and a few hundred other 'combatants' from the Labour Service and *Organisation Todt*, assigned to defend the bridges that Wenck's relieving army would have to cross. A further 5,500 sailors had been promised by Dönitz, but were not yet available. Facing them, and closing in on the city by the hour, were some 2½ million combat troops in crack divisions of the Red Army. Weidling knew from the start that his task was an impossible one.

The news from the ever-narrowing fronts around Berlin was meanwhile becoming ever grimmer. By midday on 24 April, Soviet troops from Zhukov's and Konev's armies had met up in the southern suburbs of the city. The encirclement of Busse's 9th Army was complete. Hopes of it fighting its way through to the west to join Wenck's 12th Army – still only in the preparatory stage of its march on the capital – were now illusory. Reports were reaching the Reich Chancellery of bitter street fighting in eastern and southern districts of the capital. Several districts to the north were already in Soviet hands, and the Nauen road, the last main road to the west, was blocked by T34 tanks. Tempelhof aerodrome, close to the city centre, had been bombarded by Soviet artillery since lunchtime. By the evening, Gatow airfield on the banks of the Havel to the west of Berlin had also come under heavy shelling. The East-West Axis, where Albert Speer had landed the previous day, was in practice now Berlin's last remaining thin artery of non-telephonic communication with the outside world.

By dawn next morning, areas close to the city centre had started to come under persistent and intense artillery fire. Around midday, the spearhead of Konev's army, skirting round Berlin to the south, met up with forward units from Zhukov's army, heading round the city to the north, at Ketzin in the west. Berlin was as good as encircled. About the same time, Soviet and American troops were smoking cigarettes together at Torgau, on the Elbe, in central Germany. The Reich was now cut in two.

Symbolically – there was absolutely no military purpose to the operation (other than striking at the possible focus of continued Nazi guerrilla warfare after formal cessation of hostilities from what transpired to be a mythical 'National Redoubt') – Hitler's alpine palace, the Berghof, above Berchtesgaden, had been reduced to smouldering ruins by RAF bombers that morning.

In his ever more isolated and beleaguered underground lair, with communications rapidly worsening, and with operational charts increasingly out of date and almost immediately overtaken by events, Hitler was still sure that he knew best. 'The situation in Berlin looks worse than it is,' he stated, with apparent confidence, on 25 April, having not ventured out of doors for five days. He ordered the city combed for all possible last reserves of manpower to throw into the fray and help prepare the ground from within for the arrival of Wenck. By this time, Wenck had made some advance towards the lakes south of Potsdam. But parts of his army were still engaged in combat with the Americans to the west, on the Elbe north of Wittenberg. And only remnants were by now left of the 9th Army, which was to have joined forces with him. With what he had at his disposal, Wenck had only the remotest chance of reaching Berlin.

But Wenck was now the only hope. Hitler was still looking for one final victory, one last chance to turn the tables on his enemies. Even now, he clung to the belief that the Alliance against him would fall apart if he could deliver a stinging blow to the Red Army. 'I think the moment has come when out of self-preservation-drive the others will confront in any case this hugely swollen proletarian Bolshevik colossus and moloch . . . If I can be successful here and hold the capital, perhaps the hope will grow among the English and Americans that they could maybe still face this whole danger together with a Nazi

Germany. And the only man for this is me,' he asserted.

His comments to Goebbels that day were in part still apparently directed at convincing himself that his decision not to go to southern Germany and to stay in Berlin was the right one. 'I'd regard it as a thousand times more cowardly to commit suicide on the Obersalzberg than to stand and fall here,' he stated. 'They shouldn't say: "You, as the Führer . . ." I'm only the Führer as long as I can lead. And I can't lead through sitting somewhere on a mountain, but have to have authority over armies that obey. Let me win a victory here, however difficult and tough, then I've a right again to do away with the sluggish elements who are constantly causing an obstruction. Then I'll work with the generals who've proved themselves.'

More than anything, Hitler's words were aimed at his place in history. Even now, Hitler – egged on, naturally, by Goebbels – remained the propagandist, looking to image. Whether leading to glorious victory, or sacrificial self-destruction, the last stand in the bunker was necessary for prestige purposes. It never occurred to him to question the continued slaughter of soldiers and civilians to that end. 'Only here can I attain a success,' he told Goebbels, '. . . and even if it's only a moral one, it's at least the possibility of saving face and winning time.' 'Only through a heroic attitude can we survive this hardest of times,' he went on. If he won the 'decisive battle' he would be 'rehabilitated'. It would prove by example that he had been right in dismissing generals for not holding their ground.

And if he were to lose, then he would have perished 'decently', not like some 'inglorious refugee sitting in Berchtesgaden and issuing useless orders from there'. He saw, he said, 'a possibility of repairing history' through gaining a success. 'It's the only chance to restore personal reputation . . . If we leave the world stage in disgrace, we'll have lived for nothing. Whether you continue your life a bit longer or not is completely immaterial. Rather end the struggle in honour than continue in shame and dishonour a few months or years longer.' Goebbels, with Frederick the Great's exploits at the famous Battle of Leuthen – the Prussian King's epic victory in 1757 over an Austrian army far superior in numbers – tripping once more from his tongue, summed up the 'heroic' alternatives: 'If all goes well, then it's in any case good. If things don't go well and the Führer finds in Berlin an honourable death and Europe were to become bolshevized, then in five years at the latest the Führer would be a legendary personality and National Socialism would have attained mythical status (*ein Mythos*) . . .'

III

Not everyone in the maze of tunnels below the Reich Chancellery was looking to share the 'heroic' end that Hitler and Goebbels were contemplating. 'I don't want to die with that lot down there in the bunker,' thirty-one-year-old Major Bernd von Freytag-Loringhoven, Krebs's tall adjutant, uttered. 'When it comes to the end, I want my head above ground and free.' Even the SS guards from Hitler's bodyguard were anxiously asking about Wenck's progress, consoling themselves with drink when off duty, and looking for possible exit-routes from what looked more and more like a certain underground grave. In the streets above, despite the threat – often carried out – of summary execution by 'flying courts-martial' for 'defeatism', let alone desertion, many elderly Volkssturm men, aware of the utter futility of carrying on such a hopeless unequal fight and looking to avoid a pointless 'hero's' death, sought any opportunity at the approach of Soviet troops to melt away and try to rejoin families taking what refuge they could in cellars and bunkers.

Amid the burning ruins of the great city, living conditions were deteriorating rapidly. Food was running out. The water-supply system had broken down. The old, infirm, wounded, women and children, injured soldiers, refugees, all clung on to life in the cellars, in packed shelters, and in underground stations as hell raged overhead.

As communications increasingly petered out – the lines to Jodl at OKH headquarters went dead for a time in the course of the evening – 'intelligence' of troop movements in the city was gathered for the once-mighty Army High Command in the bunker by using the telephone directory to ring numbers at random. 'Excuse me, madam, have you seen the Russians?' ran the question. 'Yes,' would come a reply, 'half an hour ago two of them were here. They were part of a group of about a dozen tanks at the cross-roads.'

Despite the uneven contest, the regular troops, mostly insufficiently trained and badly equipped, often down to their last reserves of ammunition, continued the bitter struggle in Berlin's streets. By the evening of 26 April, Soviet soldiers were close to Alexanderplatz, the very heart of the city. The Reich Chancellery in the government district, under heavy fire all day, was now less than a mile away.

A fresh moment of excitement gripped the inmates of the bunker during the early evening: the unexpected arrival of the wounded Colonel-General of the Luftwaffe Robert Ritter von Greim, propped up by his glamorous female companion, twenty years his junior, the flying-ace and test pilot Hanna Reitsch. Both were fervent, long-standing admirers of Hitler. Greim had been summoned two days earlier to Berlin. He and Reitsch had had to risk an extremely hazardous flight from Munich. Greim's foot had been injured when their Fieseler Storch had been hit by artillery fire on approach to the centre of Berlin, and Reitsch had grabbed the controls and brought the plane down safely on the East-West Axis. They had then requisitioned a car to bring them to the Reich

Chancellery. Propped up by Reitsch, the wounded Greim now limped painfully into the bunker. He still did not know why he had come.

Once his foot had been bandaged, Hitler came in to tell him. After railing at Göring's 'betrayal', Hitler informed Greim that he was promoting him to Field-Marshal and appointing him as the new head of the Luftwaffe. It could all have been done by telephone. Instead, Greim had had to risk life and limb to receive the news in person. And, it seemed likely, he and Reitsch were now doomed to end their lives in the bunker. But far from being infuriated or depressed, or both, Greim and Reitsch were exhilarated. They begged to stay in the bunker with Hitler. They were given phials of poison, should the worst happen. But Hitler persuaded Greim that all was not lost. 'Just don't lose faith,' Koller heard Greim say, when he telephoned the bunker. 'It'll all come to a good end. The meeting with the Führer and his vigour have given me extraordinary new strength. It's like the fountain of youth (*Jungbad*) here'. Koller thought it sounded more like a mad-house.

The briefing sessions were by this time much reduced in size and changed in character. Krebs was now the only senior military figure present. Goebbels had joined since taking up residence in the bunker. Hitler Youth Leader Axmann, General Weidling (responsible for the defence of Berlin), Vice-Admiral Voß (Dönitz's liaison), Colonel Nicolaus von Below (the long-serving Luftwaffe adjutant), and SS-

Brigadeführer Wilhelm Mohnke, just appointed by Hitler as commandant of the government quarter of Berlin (which had been dubbed 'The Citadel') were also present.

Discussion at the first meeting on 27 April, in the early hours, centred on the prospects of Wenck breaking through. He had reached the outskirts of Potsdam. But he had only three divisions at his disposal. He desperately needed reinforcements. The chances of Busse's beleaguered 9th Army forcing their way north-westwards to join him were now slim in the extreme. But there were still hopes that troops under Lieutenant-General Rudolf Holste, to the north-west of Berlin, might fight their way south to link up with Wenck. Time was short. Krebs reported heavy street-fighting in the heart of the city. The Soviets had advanced on Alexanderplatz. They would soon have Potsdamer Platz in their sights; and that was where the bunker was situated. 'May God let Wenck come!' intoned Goebbels. 'A dreadful situation crosses my mind,' he added, grimly. 'Wenck is located at Potsdam, and here the Soviets are pressing on Potsdamer Platz!' 'And I'm not in Potsdam, but in Potsdamer Platz,' commented Hitler, laconically.

His assessment of the situation was realistic: Wenck's three divisions were not enough. They might suffice to take Potsdam, but they were only infantry divisions, lacking panzer support, and not capable of breaking their way through the Soviet tank units. Voß breathed encouragement. 'Wenck will get here, my Führer! It's only a question of whether he can do it alone.' It was enough for Hitler to lapse into a new reverie. 'You've got to imagine. That'll spread like wildfire through the whole of Berlin when it's known: a German army has broken through in the west and established contact with the Citadel (*Festung*).' The Soviets, he thought, had suffered great losses, were suffering even more in the intense house-to-house fighting, and could only throw more troops into exposed forward positions. The thought sufficed: he had convinced himself that the situation was not wholly bleak. The constant explosions had kept him awake in recent nights. But he would sleep better tonight, he said. He only wanted to be awakened 'if a Russian tank is standing in front of my cabin' so that he had time to do what was necessary.

The second briefing of the day began with Mohnke announcing that the first enemy tanks had managed to penetrate to the Wilhelmsplatz, the heart of the government quarter. They had been repulsed – on this occasion – but time was running out. Krebs reckoned the bunker residents had no more than about twenty-four to twenty-six hours; the link-up between the armies of Wenck and Busse had to take place within that time if there was to be any hope. Hitler inwardly knew, however, that this would not happen. He repeatedly bemoaned 'the catastrophic mistake' of the 9th Army, which he blamed for ignoring his orders and trying to penetrate the Soviet lines in the wrong direction. The faint hopes from the remaining forces in the north, those of Holste and Steiner (in whom Hitler had lost all confidence days earlier), were now also – realistically, if not in dreams – largely abandoned.

Despite a desperate plea from Keitel to throw everything into the relief of Berlin, Jodl had diverted the hard-pressed units of Holste and Steiner to fend off Soviet forces to the north of the capital. It was tantamount to giving up on Berlin. Bormann scathingly commented in his diary, in remarks point-edly directed at Reichsführer-SS Himmler's recog-nized reluctance to deploy Steiner's SS corps to help save Berlin: 'The divisions marching to our relief are held up by Himmler-Jodl! *We* will stand and fall with the Führer: loyal into death. Others believe they have to act "from *higher* insight". They sacrifice the Führer, and their lack of loyalty – shame on them – matches their "feeling of honour".'

Hitler and Goebbels relapsed into reminiscences. They were prompted by Mohnke's remark, entirely without irony: 'We haven't quite brought about what we wanted in 1933, my Führer!' Hitler's explanation – it had scarcely been in his mind at the time – was that he had come to power too early. A year or more later, at Hindenburg's death, would have been the right time. To bring about a complete revolution, the old system needed to have revealed itself as utterly bankrupt. As it was, he had been forced to compro-mise with Hugenberg, Schleicher – not much of a compromise since the former Reich Chancellor had, in fact, been murdered by Hitler's henchmen at the time of the 'Röhm affair' in 1934 – and other pillars of the old order. By the time of Hindenburg's death, Hitler went on, the determination to rid himself of the conservatives had lessened, and the work of reconstruction was under way. 'Otherwise, thousands would have been eliminated at that time,' he declared. 'It could have happened, if I had come to power through an express will of the people' – presumably meaning a presidential election – 'or through a putsch. You regret it afterwards that you are so good,' he concluded.

This took the discussion inexorably once more back into pathos and an evocation of 'heroism'. He was staying in Berlin, Hitler said, 'so that I have more moral right to act against weakness . . . I can't constantly threaten others if I run away myself from the Reich capital at the critical hour . . . I've had the right to command in this city. Now I must obey the commands of fate. Even if I could save myself, I won't do it. The captain also goes down with his ship.' Voß, predictably, picked up the metaphor. Pathos and emotion got the better of him, too. 'Here in the Reich Chancellery it's just like the command-bridge of a ship,' he implausibly ruminated. 'One thing here applies to all. We don't want to get away.' (He would, ultimately, like most of the others, nevertheless seek to flee the bunker at the last moment.) 'We belong together. It's only a matter of being an upright community.'

IV

The news trickling in during the day could scarcely have been worse. Wenck's troops, without assistance from the 9th Army (whose encirclement was by now accepted as practically a foregone conclusion), had been pushed back south of Potsdam. There was a 'doomsday' mood in the bunker, alleviated only by copious supplies of alcohol and food from the Reich Chancellery cellars. Hitler told Below he had decided to give Weidling, the Commandant of Berlin, the order to break out. All his staff should go, as well as Bormann and Goebbels. He would stay behind and die in the capital. By evening, amid worsening news, he had changed his mind. An attempt to break out would be useless. He gave Below a poison-capsule, should it come to 'a difficult situation'.

The fate of the encircled 9th Army, with its eleven divisions almost four times as strong as the forces at Wenck's disposal, took Hitler back, like a long-playing record, at the third briefing of the day to what he saw as constant disobedience and disloyalty in the army. Only Schörner, commander of Army Group Centre, was singled out for praise as 'a true warlord'. Dönitz, too, stood in high favour for holding to his promise to send naval units to the defence of Berlin, and to Hitler's personal protection. The faint hope in Wenck was still not totally extinguished. But Hitler was looking to the last stand in the 'Citadel'. Firm command and reliable troops for the defence of the 'Citadel' were vital. His fear of capture surfaced again. 'I must have the absolute certainty,' he said, following news that enemy tanks had for a short time forced their way into Wilhelmstraße, 'that I will not be dragged out through some crafty trick by a Russian tank.' He saw it as only a question of time before the Soviets brought up heavy artillery to shell the 'Citadel' from close range. 'It's a matter then of a heroic struggle for a last small island,' he commented. 'If the relief doesn't arrive, we have to be clear: it's no bad end to a life to fall in the struggle for the capital of your Reich.'

Not everyone was willing to join a suicide pact. Hermann Fegelein, the swashbuckling, womanizing, cynical opportunist who had risen to high position in the SS through Himmler's favour then sealed his bonds to Hitler's 'court' through marrying Eva Braun's sister, had disappeared from the bunker. His absence was noticed on 27 April. And that evening he was discovered in civilian clothes in his apartment in Charlottenburg, allegedly with a woman friend, worse for wear from drink, and with a good deal of money in bags packed for departure. He rang Eva Braun to have his sister-in-law intercede. (It seems, in fact, that he may have been more attracted to Eva Braun than he was to her sister; and that he had been in touch with her beforehand from his apartment, attempting to persuade her to leave the bunker before it was too late.) But it was to no avail. He was hauled back into the Reich Chancellery that evening in deep disgrace, stripped of his epaulettes and collar flashes, reduced to the ranks, and kept in an improvised cell until Hitler was ready to see him.

In the early hours of 28 April, despairing calls were made from the bunker to Keitel and Jodl urging all conceivable effort to be made to relieve Berlin as absolute priority. Time was of the essence. There were at most forty-eight hours, it was thought. 'If no help comes within that time, it will be too late,' Krebs told Keitel. 'The Führer passes that on again!!!' From Wenck, there was nothing but silence.

As so often, the bunker inmates thought they smelled the scent of disloyalty and treason. Bormann telegraphed Puttkamer that evening: 'Instead of spurring on the troops who should liberate us with orders and appeals, the men in authority are silent. Loyalty has given way to disloyalty. We remain here. The Reich Chancellery is already a heap of ruins.' In his desk diary, the entry was of high treason and betrayal of the country.

An hour later, the suspicions seemed dramatically confirmed. Heinz Lorenz appeared in the bunker. He had just picked up a message from Reuters, sent by the BBC in London and confirmed in Stockholm. He gave one copy to Bormann, whom he found sitting with Goebbels and Hewel. The other copy he handed to Linge to pass on to Hitler. It confirmed the truth of a disturbing story broadcast in the morning news of Radio Stockholm, relayed to Hitler in mid-afternoon, though initially seeming to lack substance: that the Reichsführer-SS, Heinrich Himmler, had offered to surrender to the western Allies, but that this had been declined. Hitler had at first received the news, late that afternoon, of Himmler's discussions about capitulation 'with complete contempt'. He had immediately telephoned Admiral Dönitz, who had said he knew nothing of it. Dönitz then in turn contacted Himmler, who categorically denied the report and recommended ignoring it rather than putting out a denial on the radio. But Hitler continued to brood on it. Perhaps he was expecting something of the sort. His distrust of Himmler had grown in recent weeks. The disobedience, as he saw it, of Sepp Dietrich in Hungary and of Felix Steiner in the failure to attempt the relief of Berlin, showed, it seemed, that even the SS were now disloyal to him. As the day wore on, so it appeared to Below, Hitler's bitterness towards Himmler mounted.

And now it all fell into place: the earlier story had been correct, and Himmler's denial a lie. More than that: the Reuter report had added that 'Himmler had informed the western Allies that he could implement an unconditional surrender and support it.' It amounted to an implication that the Reichsführer-SS was now *de facto* head of state, that Hitler had been disempowered. This was a bombshell. This could on no account be tolerated. This was base treason.

Whether Hitler had earlier been aware of Himmler's tentative feelers towards the western powers through the intermediacy of Count Folke

Bernadotte, Vice-President of the Swedish Red Cross and a close relative of the King of Sweden, is uncertain. The Reichsführer's dealings with Bernadotte had stretched back some two months. SS-Brigadeführer Walter Schellenberg, head of the Foreign Intelligence Service in the Reich Security Main Office, had instigated the meetings and acted as intermediary. Bernadotte's initial aim had been to bargain for the release of prisoners – particularly Scandinavians – from concentration camps. From Himmler's point of view, urged on by Schellenberg, Bernadotte offered a possible opening to the West. As Germany's military situation had drastically deteriorated, Himmler, still hesitant and evidently under great nervous strain, had become more amenable to gestures at humanitarian concessions aimed at showing himself in as good a light as possible. Like most Nazi leaders, he was looking to survive, not throw himself on the funeral pyre in the Berlin *Götterdämmerung*. In March, he had agreed, in contravention of Hitler's wishes, to allow concentration camps to be handed over to the approaching enemy, not destroyed. He had conceded the release of small numbers of Jews and other prisoners, to be sent to Switzerland and Sweden. At his second meeting with Bernadotte at the beginning of April, he had also consented to let Danish and Norwegian women and the sick in camps be taken to Sweden. At the same time, he still regarded the camp prisoners as his 'hostages' – bargaining counters in any negotiations with the West.

Bernadotte had brushed aside Schellenberg's suggestion – almost certainly prompted by Himmler – that he might sound out Eisenhower about the possibility of a surrender in the West. Such a proposition, Bernadotte had pointed out, had to come from the Reichsführer himself. Himmler was, however, in a state of chronic indecision as well as extreme nervous tension. He saw clearly the writing on the wall; the war was irredeemably lost. But he was well aware that Hitler would take Germany down into perdition with him rather than capitulate. Himmler, in common with most Nazi leaders, wanted to save his own skin. And he still hankered after some role in a post-Hitler settlement. As dogmatic as Hitler in the fight against Bolshevism, he harboured the notable illusion that the enemy might overlook his part in monstrous crimes against humanity because of his value to the continuation of the struggle against the mortal enemy not just of Germany, but also of the West. He could not, however, even now free himself from his bonds with Hitler. He still hankered after Hitler's favour, and was distressed at the way he had fallen into discredit after his failure as commander of Army Group Vistula. Not least: now, as before, he feared Hitler.

A third meeting with Bernadotte on 21 April, at which the Reichsführer-SS looked extremely drawn and in a highly nervous state, made no progress on the issue of overtures to the West. Himmler still remained ultra-cautious, unwilling to risk any initiative. Possibly, as Schellenberg later suggested, he had already decided by lunchtime on 22 April that the time had come to act, though this seems doubtful. What certainly convinced him was the news which Fegelein telephoned through to him from the Führer Bunker that day of Hitler's extraordinary fit of pent-up fury and his uncontrolled tirade against treachery on all sides – not least directed at the SS on account of Steiner's failure to launch the ordered counter-offensive – culminating in his announcement that he would stay and die in Berlin. At this, Himmler's indecision evaporated.

On 23 April, Count Bernadotte had agreed, somewhat reluctantly, to Schellenberg's suggestion to meet Himmler for a fourth time that evening. The meeting took place in the Swedish Consulate in Lübeck, eerily lit by candles because of a power cut. 'Hitler is very probably already dead,' Himmler began. At any rate, his end could be no more than a few days away. Before now, his oath of loyalty had prevented him from acting, Himmler went on. But with Hitler dead or on the verge of death, the situation was different. He now had a free hand. There could be no surrender to the Soviet Union. He was, and always would be, the sworn enemy of Bolshevism. He insisted that the struggle against Bolshevism must continue. But he was ready to declare Germany defeated by the western powers, and begged Bernadotte to pass his offer of capitulation to General Eisenhower in order to prevent further senseless destruction. Still by candlelight, Himmler drafted a letter to Sweden's Foreign Minister, to be handed to him by Bernadotte, and passed on to the western Allies.

Himmler, like Göring (if in a different way), had taken the news of Hitler's outburst on 22 April to imply the Führer's effective abdication. Like Göring, Himmler was soon to be disabused of such presumption. His immediate instinct, however, now that his own decision had been clarified, was to build a cabinet, invent (at Schellenberg's suggestion) the name for a new party – the 'Party of National Concentration (*Nationale Sammlungspartei*)' – and ponder whether he should bow or shake hands when he met Eisenhower. It apparently never occurred to him that his offer of capitulation might be turned down. But that outcome – as good as certain to all beyond the perimeters of the detached mental world of Nazi leaders at this juncture – was precisely what had happened by the time, during the course of the afternoon of 28 April, the sensational news filtered out of the Reichsführer-SS's willingness to capitulate.

For Hitler, this was the last straw. That his 'loyal Heinrich', whose SS had as its motto 'my honour is loyalty', should now stab him in the back: this was the end. It was the betrayal of all betrayals. The bunker reverberated to a final elemental explosion of fury. All his stored-up venom was now poured out on Himmler in a last paroxysm of seething rage. It was, he screamed, 'the most shameful betrayal in human history.'

When the outburst subsided, Hitler retired to his rooms with Goebbels and Bormann for a lengthy discussion. As soon as he reappeared, he sent for the imprisoned Fegelein and subjected him to a fearsome verbal assault. Fegelein's recent disappearance now appeared to have sinister significance: joining the base treachery of the Reichsführer-SS. Hitler's paranoid suspicions were running riot. Possibly Himmler was plotting to assassinate him; or to hand him over to the enemy. And Fegelein was part of the plot. After the merest formalities in a hastily improvised 'court martial', Fegelein was summarily sentenced to death, immediately taken out, put in front of a firing-squad and executed. For some of the bunker inmates, there was a sense of shock that one from within the 'inner circle' was guilty of such 'betrayal', and had been so peremptorily dispatched. For Hitler, it was the closest he could come to revenge on the Reichsführer-SS himself.

V

By now, Soviet troops had forced their way into Potsdamer Platz and streets in the immediate vicinity of the Reich Chancellery. They were no more than a few hundred yards away. A breakdown in communications for most of the day had left the bunker inmates desperate for any news of Wenck's army (which remained, hemmed in, south of Potsdam). In the prevailing climate within the bunker, even the lapdog Keitel and the ever-reliable Jodl were now coming under suspicion of treachery for not bringing about the relief of Berlin.

Soon after midnight, following Fegelein's execution, Hitler commissioned Greim to deploy the Luftwaffe in making every effort to aid Wenck through attacks on Soviet positions blocking his route to Berlin. It was the faintest of faint hopes. He had a second commission for Greim – one, if anything, even more important. Greim was to leave Berlin and fly to Dönitz in Plön to ensure that the traitor, Himmler, was arrested – better still, liquidated forthwith. To this end, an Arado 96 training plane had been ordered to Berlin from Rechlin and, astonishingly, had defied all odds in touching down on the East-West Axis. Protesting their wish to stay with Hitler in the bunker, Greim, on crutches and far from recovered from his injured foot, and his companion Hanna Reitsch nonetheless accepted the commission, were driven in an armoured vehicle to the plane, waiting close to the Brandenburg Gate, managed to take off, and, even more remarkably, to negotiate the heavy Soviet anti-aircraft fire to fly to Rechlin, from where they later flew to Plön. The perilous journey was pointless. The few planes Greim was able to order into the defence of Berlin made not the slightest difference. And by the time he reached Dönitz's headquarters, the Grand Admiral had nothing to gain by having Himmler arrested, let alone shot. Even avoiding death in the bunker was no consolation to Greim and Reitsch. 'It is the greatest sorrow of our lives that we were not permitted to die with the Führer,' they chorused some days later. 'One should kneel in reverence at the altar of the Fatherland and pray.'

After Greim and Reitsch had left, Hitler became calmer. It was time to make preparations. As long as Hitler had had a future, he had ruled out marriage. His life, he had said, was devoted to Germany. There was no room for a wife. It had also been politically inconvenient. No one outside the inner circle was to know of Eva Braun's existence. She had been forced to accept that she was no more than an appendage, there when Hitler wanted her to be, stored well out of sight for the rest of the time. But she had chosen to come to the bunker. And she had refused Hitler's own entreaties to leave. She had committed herself to him once and for all, when others were deserting. The marriage now cost him nothing. He did it simply to please Eva Braun, to give her what she had wanted more than anything at a moment when marrying him was the least enviable fate in the world.

Eva Braun had dropped a hint earlier in the day that this would be her wedding night. Now, following the departure of Greim and Reitsch, not long after midnight on 29 April, in the most macabre surroundings, with the bunker shaking from nearby explosions, Hitler and Eva Braun exchanged marriage vows in the conference-room in front of one of Goebbels's minor officials, city councillor Walter Wagner, dressed in Nazi uniform with a Volkssturm armband, who had been brought to the bunker in an armoured car to conduct the bizarre ceremony. Goebbels and Bormann were witnesses. The rest of the staff waited outside to congratulate the newly wedded couple. Champagne, sandwiches, and reminiscences – with somewhat forced joviality – of happier days followed.

Just before the wedding ceremony, Hitler had asked his youngest secretary, Traudl Junge, to go with him to the room where his military conferences took place. It had been about 11.30 p.m. when he said that he wanted her to take down some dictation. She was still wondering what this might be at such a late hour when, leaning on the table, he started to dictate his last will and testament.

He began with a brief Private Testament. He referred first to his marriage to Eva Braun, and her decision to come to Berlin and die at his side. He disposed of his possessions to the Party – or, should it no longer exist, to the state; he still hoped his collection of paintings would go to a gallery in Linz; and he appointed Martin Bormann as executor to see that relatives and his long-serving staff had some reward for their support.

He came to the more significant part. 'This is my political testament,' he declared. Traudl Junge paused for a moment, expectantly. But she had heard it all before. His last words for posterity were a piece of pure self-justification. The rhetoric is instantly

recognizable, redolent of *Mein Kampf* and countless
speeches; the central idea of the responsibility of
international Jewry for the death, suffering, and
destruction in the war remained unchanged, even as
he himself now looked death in the face. 'It is untrue
that I or anyone else in Germany wanted the war in
1939,' he dictated. 'It was desired and instigated exclusively by those international statesmen who were
either of Jewish descent or who worked for Jewish
interests . . . Centuries will pass away, but out of the
ruins of our towns and cultural monuments the
hatred will ever renew itself against those ultimately
responsible whom we have to thank for everything:
international Jewry and its helpers.' The conspiracy
theory continued unabated. He attributed the rejec-
tion of his proposal on the eve of the attack on Poland
partly to the business interests of 'leading circles in
English politics', partly to the 'influence of propaganda organized by international Jewry'.

He came to a key passage – an oblique reference
to the 'Final Solution' – relating once more to the
fulfilment of the 'prophecy,' of 1939: 'I also left no
doubt that, if the nations of Europe are again to be
regarded as mere blocks of shares of these international money and finance conspirators, then that
race, too, which is really guilty of this murderous
struggle, will be called to account: Jewry! I further
left no one in doubt that this time millions of children of Europe's aryan peoples would not die of
hunger, millions of grown men would not suffer

death, and hundreds of thousands of women and children not be burnt and bombed to death in the towns, without the real culprit having to atone for his guilt, even if by my more humane means.'

Despite all its setbacks, the six-year struggle, he went on, would one day go down in history as 'the most glorious and valiant manifestation of a nation's will to existence'. He himself could not forsake Berlin. The forces there were too small to hold out against the enemy and – the inevitable side-swipe against those deemed to have betrayed him – 'our own resistance is gradually devalued by deluded and characterless subjects'. He would choose death at the appropriate moment.

Again, he gave an indication of his own fear of what he saw as the still dominant power of the Jews: 'I do not wish to fall into the hands of enemies who, for the amusement of their whipped-up masses, will need a spectacle arranged by Jews.'

A renaissance of National Socialism, he avowed, would eventually emerge from the sacrifice of the soldiers and his own death alongside them. He ended with an exhortation to continue the struggle. He begged the heads of the armed forces to instil the spirit of National Socialism in the troops. His long-standing scapegoat, the officer corps of the army, did not even now go unscathed: 'May it at some time be part of the concept of honour of the German officer – as is already the case in our navy – that the surrender of a district or a town is impossible and that above all the leaders have to proceed here with a shining example in most loyal fulfilment of their duty unto death.'

In the second part of his Testament, Hitler went through the charade of nominating a successor government for what was left of the Reich. The tone was vindictive. Göring and Himmler were formally expelled from the Party and from all their offices for the damage they had done through negotiating with the enemy 'without my knowledge and against my wishes', for attempting to take power in the state, and for disloyalty to his person. Nor was there any place in the new government for Speer. The new head of state and head of the armed forces was Grand Admiral Dönitz – less of a surprise than at first sight, given his specially high standing in Hitler's eyes in the closing phase of the war, and in view particularly of the responsibility he had already been given a few days earlier for Party and state affairs as well as military matters in the northern part of the country. Significantly, however, Dönitz was not to inherit the title of Führer. Instead, the title of Reich President, dropped in 1934 on Hindenburg's death, was reinvented. Goebbels, who had been pressing for so long for full control over internal affairs, was rewarded for his loyalty by being appointed Chancellor of a Reich that scarcely any longer existed. Bormann, another who had proved his loyalty, was made Party Minister. Goebbels – who, together with Bormann, kept bringing Fräulein

Junge the names of further ministers for typing in the list – probably engineered the dismissal at this late point of his old adversary Ribbentrop, and his replacement as Foreign Minister by Arthur Seyß-Inquart. Hitler's favourite general, Schörner, was to be Commander of the Army, while Gauleiter Karl Hanke, still holding out in Breslau, was to take over from Himmler as Reichsführer-SS and Chief of the German Police. The tough Munich Gauleiter, Paul Giesler, was made Interior Minister, with Karl-Otto Saur replacing Speer as Minister for Armaments. The pointless job of Propaganda Minister fell to Goebbels's State Secretary, Werner Naumann. Old survivors included Schwerin-Krosigk (Finance), Funk (Economics), Thierack (Justice), and Herbert Backe (Agriculture). Hitler commissioned them with continuing the task – 'the work of coming centuries' – of building up a National Socialist State. 'Above all,' the Political Testament concluded, 'I charge the leadership of the nation and their subjects (*Gefolgschaft*) with the meticulous observance of the race-laws and the merciless resistance to the universal poisoner of all peoples, international Jewry.'

It was turned 4 a.m. when Goebbels, Bormann, Burgdorf, and Krebs signed the Political Testament, and Nicolaus von Below added his signature to the Private Testament.

Hitler, looking weary, took himself off to rest. He had completed the winding-up order on the Third Reich. Only the final act of self-destruction remained.

For Fräulein Junge, however, the night's secretarial duties were not yet over. Soon after Hitler had retired, Goebbels, in a highly emotional state, white-faced, tears running down his cheeks, appeared in the ante-room, where she was finishing her work. He asked her to draft his own coda to Hitler's will. Hitler, he said, had ordered him to leave Berlin as a member of the new government. But 'if the Führer is dead, my life is meaningless', he told her. Of all the Nazi leaders, Goebbels was the one who for weeks had assessed with some realism the military prospects, had repeat-edly evoked the imagery of heroism, looking to his own place in the pantheon of Teutonic heroes, and had accordingly brought his wife and children to the bunker to die alongside their adored Leader in a final act of *Nibelungentreue*. It was, therefore, utterly consis-tent when he now dictated: 'For the first time in my life, I must categorically refuse to obey an order of the Führer.' His wife and children joined him in this refusal. He would, he continued, lose all self-respect – quite apart from the demands of personal loyalty – were he to 'leave the Führer alone in his hour of greatest need'. Betrayal was in his mind, as in that of his master. 'In the delirium of treachery, which surrounds the Führer in these critical days of the war,' he had Fräulein Junge type, 'there have to be at least a few who stay unconditionally loyal to him even unto death, even if this contradicts a formal, objectively well-founded order which finds expression in his Political Testament.' Consequently, he – together with his wife and children (who, were they old enough to judge, would be in agreement) – were firmly resolved not to leave the Reich capital 'and rather at the Führer's side to end a life which for me personally has no further value if it cannot be used in the service of the Führer and by his side'. It was 5.30 a.m. before this last act in the nocturnal drama closed.

VI

The mood in the bunker now sank to zero-level. Despair was now written on everyone's face. All knew it was only a matter of hours before Hitler killed himself, and wondered what the future held for them after his death. There was much talk of the best methods of committing suicide. Secretaries, adjutants, and any others who wanted them had by now been given the brass-cased ampoules containing prussic acid supplied by Dr Ludwig Stumpfegger, the SS surgeon who had joined the 'court' the previous October. Hitler's paranoia stretched now to doubts about the capsules. He had shown his alsatian bitch Blondi more affection in recent years than any human being, probably including even Eva Braun. Now, as the end approached, he had the poison tested on Blondi. Professor Werner Haase was summoned from his duties in the nearby public air-raid shelter beneath the new Reich Chancellery building nearby. Shortly before the afternoon briefing on 29 April, aided by Hitler's dog-attendant, Sergeant Fritz Tornow, he forced open the dog's jaws and crushed the prussic acid capsule with a pair of pliers. The dog slumped in an instant motionless to the ground. Hitler was not present. However, he entered the room immediately afterwards. He glanced for a few seconds at the dead dog. Then, his face like a mask, he left without saying anything and shut himself in his room.

The bunker community had by this time dwindled still further. Three emissaries – Bormann's adjutant, SS-Standartenführer Wilhelm Zander, Hitler's army adjutant Major Willi Johannmeier, and Acting Press Chief Heinz Lorenz – had left that morning as couriers on a perilous, and fruitless, mission to deliver copies of the Testament to Dönitz, Schörner, and the Nazi Party's Headquarters, the 'Brown House' in Munich. By this time, normal telephone communications had finally broken down, though naval and Party telegraph wires remained usable, with difficulty, to the end. But dispatch runners brought reports that Soviet troops had brought up their lines to a mere 400–500 metres from the Reich Chancellery. The Berlin Commandant General Weidling informed Hitler that they had begun a concentrated attack on the 'Citadel'; resistance could only be sustained for a short time. Three young officers, Major Bernd von Loringhoven (Krebs's adjutant), his friend Gerhard Boldt (the Chief of Staff's orderly), and Lieutenant-Colonel Rudolf Weiß (General Burgdorf's adjutant) decided to try a last chance to escape from their predestined tomb. They put it to Krebs that they should break out in the attempt to reach Wenck. He agreed; so, following the midday conference, did Hitler. As he shook hands wearily with them, he said: 'Give my regards to Wenck. Tell him to hurry or it will be too late.'

That afternoon, Below too, who had been a member of Hitler's 'household' since 1937, decided to try his luck. He asked if Hitler would permit him to attempt to get through to the west. Hitler readily agreed. Below left late that night, bearing a letter from Hitler to Keitel which, from Below's memory of it (the letter itself was destroyed), repeated his praise for the navy, his attribution of blame for the Luftwaffe's failure exclusively to Göring, and his condemnation of the General Staff together with the disloyalty and betrayal which had for so long undermined his efforts. He could not believe, he said, that the sacrifices of the German people had been in vain. The aim had still to be the winning of territory in the East.

By this time, Hitler had learned that Mussolini had been captured and executed by Italian partisans. Whether he was told the details – how Mussolini was hanged upside down in a square in Milan, together with his mistress Clara Petacci, and stoned by a mob – is uncertain. If he did learn the full gory tale, it could have done no more than confirm his anxiety to take his own life before it was too late, and to prevent his body from being seized by his enemies. During the late-evening briefing, General Weidling had told Hitler that the Russians would reach the Reich Chancellery no later than 1 May. There was little time remaining.

Nevertheless, Hitler undertook one last attempt to ascertain the possibilities of relief, even at this late hour. With nothing heard throughout the day of Wenck's progress (or lack of it), he cabled five questions to Jodl in the most recent OKW headquarters in Dobbin at eleven o'clock that evening, asking in the tersest fashion where Wenck's spearheads were, when the attack would come, where the 9th Army was, where Holste's troops were, and when *their* attack might be expected.

Keitel's reply arrived shortly before 3 a.m. on 30 April: Wenck's army was still engaged south of the Schwielow Lake, outside Potsdam, and unable to continue its attack on Berlin. The 9th Army was encircled. The Korps Holste had been forced on to the defensive. Keitel added, below the report: 'Attacks on Berlin not advanced anywhere.' It was now plain beyond any equivocation: there would be no relief of the Reich capital.

Hitler had, in fact, already given up. Before 2 a.m. he had said goodbye to a gathering of around twenty to twenty-five servants and guards. He mentioned Himmler's treachery and told them that he had decided to take his own life rather than be captured by the Russians and put on show like an exhibition in a museum. He shook hands with each of them, thanked them for their service, released them from their oath to him, and hoped they would find their way to the British or Americans rather than fall into Russian hands. He then went through the same farewell ceremony with the two doctors, Haase and Schenck, and the nurses and assistants, who had served in the emergency hospital established below the New Reich Chancellery.

At dawn, Soviet artillery opened up intensive bombardment of the Reich Chancellery and neighbouring buildings. Hitler inquired soon afterwards of the commandant of the 'Citadel', SS-Obergruppenführer Mohnke, how long he could hold out. He was told for one to two days at most. In the last briefing, in the late morning, Berlin's commandant, General Weidling, was even more pessimistic. Munition was fast running out; air-supplies had dried up and any replenishment was out of the question; morale was at rock-bottom; the fighting was now in a very small area of the city. The battle for Berlin would in all probability, he concluded, be over that evening. After a long silence, Hitler, in a tired voice, asked Mohnke's view. The 'Citadel' commandant concurred. Hitler wearily levered himself out of his chair. Weidling pressed him for a decision on whether, in the event of a total ammunitions failure, the remaining troops could attempt to break out. Hitler spoke briefly with Krebs, then gave permission – which he confirmed in writing – for a break-out to be attempted in small numbers. As before, he rejected emphatically a capitulation of the capital.

He sent for Bormann. It was by now around noon. He told him the time had come; he would shoot himself that afternoon. Eva Braun would also commit suicide. Their bodies were to be burnt. He then summoned his personal adjutant, SS-Sturmbannführer Otto Günsche. He did not want to be put on display in some waxworks in Moscow, he said. He commissioned Günsche with making the arrangements for the cremation, and for ensuring that it was carried out according to his instructions. Hitler was calm and collected. Günsche, less calm, immediately rushed to telephone Hitler's chauffeur, Erich Kempka, to obtain as much petrol as was available. He impressed upon him the urgency. The Soviets could reach the Chancellery garden at any time.

Hitler took lunch as usual around 1 p.m. with his secretaries, Traudl Junge and Gerda Christian, and his dietician Fräulein Manziarly. Eva Braun was not present. Hitler was composed, giving no hint that his death was imminent. Some time after the meal had ended, Günsche told the secretaries that Hitler wished to say farewell to them. They joined Martin Bormann, Joseph and Magda Goebbels, General Burgdorf and General Krebs, and others from the 'inner circle' of the bunker community. Looking more stooped than ever, Hitler, dressed as usual in his uniform jacket and black trousers, appeared alongside Eva Braun, who was wearing a blue dress with white trimmings. He held out his hand to each of them, muttered a few words, and, within a few minutes and without further formalities, returned to his study.

Eva Braun went into Magda Goebbels's room with her. Magda, on whom three days earlier Hitler had pinned his own Golden Party Badge – a signal token of esteem for one of his most fervent admirers – was in a tearful state. She was conscious not only that this was the end for the Führer she revered but that within hours she would be taking, as well as her own life, the lives of her six children, still playing happily in the corridors of the bunker. Highly agitated, Magda immediately reappeared, asking Günsche to speak to Hitler again. Hitler somewhat grudgingly agreed and went in to see Magda. It was said that she begged him a last time to leave Berlin. The response was predictable and unemotional. Inside a minute, Hitler had retreated behind the doors of his study for the last time. Eva Braun followed him almost immediately. It was shortly before half past three.

For the next few minutes, Goebbels, Bormann, Axmann (who had arrived too late to say his own farewell to Hitler) and the remaining members of the bunker community waited. Günsche stood on guard outside Hitler's room. The only noise was the drone of the diesel ventilator. In the upstairs part of the bunker, Traudl Junge chatted with the Goebbels children as they ate their lunch.

After waiting ten minutes or so, still without a sound from Hitler's room, Linge took the initiative. He took Bormann with him and cautiously opened the door. In the cramped study, Hitler and Eva Braun sat alongside each other on the small sofa. Eva Braun was slumped to Hitler's left. A strong whiff of bitter almonds – the distinctive smell of prussic acid – drifted up from her body. Hitler's head drooped lifelessly. Blood dripped from a bullet-hole in his right temple. His 7.65mm Walther pistol lay by his foot.

POCKET PENGUINS